MENTAL MATHS HOMEWORK

FOR 7 YEAR OLDS

SERIES EDITOR
Lin Taylor
The IMPACT Project, University of
North London Enterprises Ltd

AUTHOR
Helen Williams

EDITOR
Joel Lane

ASSISTANT EDITOR
Clare Miller

SERIES DESIGNERS
Anna Oliwa and Rachel Warner

DESIGNER
Rachel Warner

ILLUSTRATIONS
Garry Davies

COVER ARTWORK
James Alexander/David Oliver
Berkeley Studios

Text © 1999 Helen Williams
© 1999 Scholastic Ltd

Designed using Adobe Pagemaker
Published by Scholastic Ltd, Villiers House, Clarendon
Avenue, Leamington Spa, Warwickshire CV32 5PR

1 2 3 4 5 6 7 8 9 0   9 0 1 2 3 4 5 6 7 8

British Library Cataloguing-in-Publication Data
A catalogue record for this book is available from the
British Library.

ISBN 0-439-01703-3

CONTENTS

IMPACT

ABOUT HOMEWORK

Homework can be a very useful opportunity to practise and develop children's understanding of the work done in school. Games and maths challenges can be very good activities to share with someone at home, especially to develop mental maths strategies and maths language skills. Research* indicates that parental involvement is a major factor in children's educational success. Most parents want to help their children with their school work, but often do not know how and 'traditional' homework does not involve parents. Shared homework activities, such as can be found in *Mental Maths Homework*, are designed to be completed with a parent or helper, such as a sibling, neighbour or other adult who can work with the child. Working one-to-one with an adult in the home environment really has a powerful effect. The National Numeracy Strategy strongly supports this type of homework, which is in line with a variety of government guidelines on the role of parents and making home links.

ABOUT MENTAL MATHS AT HOME

Mental Maths Homework is particularly concerned to develop children's *mental* mathematics. In order to become competent at mental calculation, children need to talk about mathematics and try out different strategies, as well as to practise number facts and skills. Children explaining their mathematics to a parent or helper can help to clarify and develop their understanding of the mathematics. This type of homework, developed by The IMPACT Project, is a *joint* activity: the helper and child working together.

ABOUT MENTAL MATHS HOMEWORK

This series comprises of six books, one for each age group from 6–11 years (Year 1/P2–Year 6/P7). Each book contains 36 photocopiable activities – enough for one to be sent home each week throughout the school year, if you wish. The activities concentrate on the number system and developing children's calculation strategies and are designed to fit into your planning, whatever scheme you are using. Since these books are designed to support the same aims of developing mental maths strategies and vocabulary, they make an ideal follow-on to the class work outlined in Scholastic's other *Mental Maths* series. The objectives for each activity are based on those in the National Numeracy Strategy *Framework for Teaching Mathematics* and the content is appropriate for teachers following other UK curriculum documents.

USING THE ACTIVITIES IN SCHOOL

Although the books are designed for a particular age group they should be used flexibly so that the right level of activity is set for a child or class. All the activities are photocopiable: most are one page, some are two, or require an extra resource page (to be found at the back of the book) for certain games or number card activities. The activities for older children will generally take longer than those for younger children.

BEFORE

It is essential that each activity is introduced to the class before it is sent home with them. This fulfils several crucial functions. It enables the child to explain the activity to the parent or carer; ensuring the child understands the task. It also familiarises the child with the activity; developing motivation and making the activity more accessible. This initial introduction to the activity can be done as part of a regular maths lesson, at the end of the day, or whenever fits in with your class's routine.

AFTER

It is also important that the child brings something back to school from the activity at home. This will not necessarily be substantial, or even anything written, since the activities aim to develop mental mathematics. It is equally important that what the child brings in from home is genuinely valued by you. It is unlikely that parents will be encouraged to share activities with their children if they do not feel that their role is valued either. Each activity indicates what should be brought back to school, and the teachers' notes (on pages 5–8) offer guidance on introducing and working with or reviewing the outcome of each activity.

HELPERS

All the activities have a note to the helper explaining the purpose of the activity and how to help the child, often emphasizing useful vocabulary. The helpers' notes also give indications of how to adapt the activity at home, and what to do if the child gets stuck. Many of the activities are games or fun activities which it is hoped that the parent and child will enjoy doing together and will do again, even when not set for homework, thus increasing the educational benefit. It is particularly beneficial for a game to be played a number of times.

OTHER WAYS TO USE THE ACTIVITIES

The activities offered in *Mental Maths Homework* are very flexible and will be used in different ways in different schools. As well as being used for shared homework, they could form the basis of a display or a school challenge, or be used as activities for a maths club. Or, they could be used independently of the school situation by parents who wish to provide stimulating and appropriate educational activities for their children.

USING THE ACTIVITIES AT HOME

If you are a parent using these activities outside of school:
● Choose an activity you both think looks interesting and get going straight away with your child. Make the work *joint*: the helper and the child working out what has to be done *together*.
● Read the instructions to your child and ask him or her to explain what has to be done. It is very effective for the child to do the explaining.

USING HOMEWORK DIARIES

Developing a dialogue between teacher and parent is an important part of shared homework. By working with the child at home, the parent becomes more familiar with the mathematics of the classroom. The teacher also needs to hear from the parent about how the child is faring with the activities. Diaries provide a very good mechanism for this. The helpers and/or the children can comment on the activities (which will give you important feedback) and individual targets can be put into the diary. The diaries can act, therefore, as an important channel of communication. (See below for details about finding out more information about diaries.)

ABOUT THIS BOOK

In *Mental Maths Homework for 7 year olds* the balance of the activities is towards 'Counting and ordering'. This is because counting and awareness of our number system underpins children's understanding of number. Counting, not only to establish quantity, but also to learn the order of the words, is crucial to understanding number. In order for the regularity in the number system to become apparent to children, they will need to do the following: count aloud regularly; count above 20, and preferably above 60 (where the aural pattern is regular, e.g. six-ty = six tens); see the numbers in position, for example on a 0–100 number line. There is very little in this book to be recorded on paper. It is certainly not appropriate to encourage 7 year olds to do any formal recording of arithmetical operations on paper. The emphasis is on discussion, developing mental strategies and searching for rules and patterns.

* Bastiani, J. & Wolfendale, S. (1996) *Home-School Work: Review, Reflection and Development* David Fulton Publishers.

THE IMPACT PROJECT

The activities in *Mental Maths Homework* have all been devised by members of The IMPACT Project, based at the University of North London. The project, a pioneer of shared homework, with a wealth of experience, is involved in a variety of initiatives concerning parental involvement and homework. It also supports schools in setting up a school framework for shared homework. If you would like help with developing shared homework, planning a whole-school framework for homework or developing mental mathematics at home and at school, maybe through INSET with experienced providers, contact The IMPACT Project. Information about other activities undertaken by the project and about other IMPACT books and resources, such as the IMPACT diaries, is also available from The IMPACT Project.

The IMPACT Project
University of North London
School of Education
166–220 Holloway Road
London
N7 8DB

tel. no. 020 7753 7052

fax. no. 020 7753 5420

e-mail: impact-enquiries@unl.ac.uk
impact-orders@unl.ac.uk

web: http://www.unl.ac.uk/impact

COUNTING & ORDERING

AFTER YOU

OBJECTIVE: To say the number names in order to at least 100.

BEFORE: Play the game with you saying one number and the group saying the next.

AFTER: Discuss the patterns in the lists of numbers the children bring into school. Count together regularly as a class or group, and counting sequentially around a circle to and from different numbers. Try saying 'ZAP' instead of the multiples of 10: '18, 19, ZAP, 21, 22...'

BACKWARDS AFTER YOU

OBJECTIVE: To say the number names in order to at least 100, from and back to zero.

BEFORE: This activity complements 'After you'. Play 'Backwards after you' using a number line as a visual aid, with you saying the starting number and the group saying the number before it.

AFTER: Count backwards for a few minutes every day, developing this to counting backwards across a ten. Discuss the patterns in the children's lists of numbers. Play the game in groups of three.

PILE OF 2PS

OBJECTIVES: To count on and back in twos from and to zero. To begin to recognize multiples of 2.

BEFORE: Remind the children of the values of different coins. Count in twos as a class, sticking 2p coins to the board with Blu-Tack as you count.

AFTER: Discuss the patterns in the children's lists of numbers; write down the numbers as they count, and discuss the 'missing' (odd) numbers; follow the count on a 0–100 number line. Repeat the homework activity, starting from different small numbers.

FILL IT WITH 10PS

OBJECTIVES: To count on and back in tens. To begin to recognize multiples of 10.

BEFORE: Model the activity, using a different shape.

AFTER: Compare the children's findings. If there were any variations in the amount the children found the shape to hold, ask them why they think this happened. Start with different amounts already inside the shape, and count on in tens each time.

THINGS IN THE RING

OBJECTIVES: To use and understand the vocabulary of estimation and approximation (such as *estimate, fewer, more, about the same as*). To give a sensible estimate of up to 50 objects.

BEFORE: Model the activity. Discuss different estimates, and how to reach a 'good' estimate.

AFTER: Compare the bags of objects that the children bring in. Repeat the activity with different items. It is important to encourage the 'glimpse' approach in order to stop the children trying to count. Discuss and compare different ways of counting efficiently (such as organizing objects into groups).

BOOK PAGES

OBJECTIVES: To round numbers to the nearest 10. To recognize multiples of 10.

BEFORE: As a class, count in 10s forwards and backwards, following the count on a number line. Find numbers that are next to, near to and in between other numbers.

AFTER: The children can use their number lists to order non-consecutive numbers. Ask questions such as *Who has a larger number?* and *Who has a number which fits between 45 and 53?* Mark the multiples of 10 on your class number line; then call out a multiple of 10 and ask the children to select two cards to make a two-digit number as near to that multiple as possible.

DOT-TO-DOT

OBJECTIVES: To order a set of non-consecutive two-digit numbers. To know what each digit in a two-digit number represents.

BEFORE: Do the preliminary activity as a class.

AFTER: Look at the completed sheets together. As an extension, the children could complete the dot-to-dot puzzles on page 46.

IMPORTANT DATES

OBJECTIVES: To use and read vocabulary related to time (such as *months, date, year, calendar*). To know the months of the year in order.

BEFORE: Work through an example, using your own birthday. Talk about calendars and the ways in which dates are written (using words or numbers).

AFTER: Discuss the dates the children bring back to school; convert them back into words and order them. If possible, write them on the class year planner. For the rest of the week, write each day's date both in numbers and in words. Talk about what will be different the next day, the next month, the next year.

POCKET MONEY

OBJECTIVES: To count on in tens from any two-digit number. To count on in different-sized steps. To use coins to add and subtract.

BEFORE: Remind the children of coin values. Count in different steps, using a number line as a visual aid.

AFTER: Discuss the children's lists of numbers. Ask them what pattern they notice, and encourage them to continue the pattern by predicting some later numbers. Enter a two-digit number into a calculator and count back in tens by repeatedly subtracting 10. Follow the same pattern on a number line.

IN A MINUTE

OBJECTIVES: To use and estimate units of time: a minute. To use numbers to solve problems.

BEFORE: As a class, watch one minute pass. Try asking the children to close their eyes and raise their hands silently when they think a minute is up.
AFTER: Compare the children's minute-activities. Discuss how they recorded their findings. Why do their results vary? If they were to repeat one of the tasks, do they think they would get the same result? Ask everyone in the class to complete the same task; make a chart of the results, and discuss it.

FILL THE BOX

OBJECTIVES: To measure and compare capacity using non-standard units. To use vocabulary related to capacity (such as *full, empty, hold, contain*). To count objects accurately by grouping them.
BEFORE: Discuss the task and the vocabulary.
AFTER: Discuss the empty containers and how much they hold. Use the same unit of measurement to compare all the containers. Ask *How large is a mini-box of Smarties?* and try filling it with different units of measurement: *How many matchsticks do you think it will hold? How many butter-beans?*

ODD DOMINOES

OBJECTIVES: To recognize odd and even numbers. To practise recall of addition and subtraction facts. To use vocabulary related to addition and subtraction (such as *total, add, difference, odd, even*).
BEFORE: Make sure the children understand the traditional domino game, perhaps using page 47. Discuss odd and even numbers.
AFTER: Replay the game with a group. Discuss their lists of odd numbers. Sort all the dominoes into those with even totals and those with odd totals.

EVEN DOMINOES

OBJECTIVES: To recognize odd and even numbers. To practise recall of addition and subtraction facts. To use vocabulary related to addition and subtraction (such as *total, add, difference, odd, even*).
BEFORE: See the notes for 'Odd Dominoes' above; the two activities are complementary.
AFTER: Replay the game with a group. Have they noticed anything about adding two odd numbers, or finding the difference between them? Is there a rule?

GET IN ORDER!

OBJECTIVES: To read, write and order consecutive numbers to 100. To know what each digit in a two-digit number represents. To use vocabulary associated with ordinal numbers (such as *less, more, before, after, last, last but one, in between*).
BEFORE: As a class, mix up and then re-order ten consecutive two-digit numbers.
AFTER: Discuss the homework. How much did the children improve their time? How could they get better? Discuss which digit they have to pay attention to when ordering. Spend a little time each day ordering different sets of numbers against the clock.

TARGET 50

OBJECTIVES: To know what each digit in a two-digit number represents. To read, compare and order non-consecutive numbers to 100.
BEFORE: Play the game as a class and discuss the numbers made.
AFTER: Ask the children about the numbers they made. How did they decide where to put their first card? Try playing the game with more players. How does this affect what happens? Discuss ways of working out how near to 50 each number is.

LOTS AND LOTS

OBJECTIVES: To use the vocabulary of estimation and approximation (such as *roughly, nearly, about the same as, too many, too few, estimate*). To round numbers less than 100 to the nearest 10. To give estimates of larger numbers.
BEFORE: This task should ideally be sent home for longer than a week, to allow the children time to collect a variety of pictures. Show them some pictures that you have collected, and explain that you are going to make a class book or display of numbers.
AFTER: Working with small groups, look at the pictures the children have brought in. Can they order the numbers? Make a class book or display. Discuss ways in which to organize the counting of a large number.

CLOCKS

OBJECTIVES: To use vocabulary related to time (such as *earliest, latest, hour, minute, second, digital, analogue*). To read and understand different ways of writing the time.
BEFORE: Discuss where to look for clocks. Draw their attention to the classroom clock at different times.
AFTER: Cut out the clocks the children have drawn and arrange them in time order on a 'washing line'. Ask the children to draw what happens at each time.

ADDITION & SUBTRACTION

SUBTRACT TO WIN

OBJECTIVES: To predict the result of several subtractions, using known subtraction facts. To solve a mathematical puzzle.
BEFORE: Play the game once (you against the class). Briefly discuss what happens.
AFTER: Play the game several times in threes, then discuss strategies for winning. Play 'Count to 21': pairs count consecutively, taking turns to say either one or two numbers. The player who says '21' wins.

FOLDING FINGERS

OBJECTIVES: To know the pairs of numbers that add up to 10. To know the pairs of multiples of 10 that add up to 100.

BEFORE: As a class, find the pairs of numbers that total ten using fingers.

AFTER: Discuss the children's lists of pairs of numbers that total 100. Rewrite them in order, then ask the children to describe the pattern of the numbers. Display it; every day, cover one number on the list for the children to name.

THREE-DICE ADDITION

OBJECTIVE: To add three single-digit numbers mentally to make 20. To know that addition can be done in any order.

BEFORE: Practise finding the total of three numbers by rolling three dice. Check that the children will be able to find three dice at home – if not, perhaps dice could be lent to them.

AFTER: Discuss the game and observe the children playing. Discuss quick ways of adding three numbers, such as counting on from the largest, or adding a pair that you know and then adding on the third number.

DIFFERENCE DOMINOES

OBJECTIVE: To use known subtraction facts. To use vocabulary related to subtraction (such as *difference, between*). To choose an appropriate operation and think logically.

BEFORE: Make sure the children understand the traditional domino game, perhaps using the dominoes on page 47. Remind the children what the word 'difference' means as a mathematical term. Make sure that they can explain this to their helpers.

AFTER: Replay the game with a group and ask them to explain how they decide which domino to place. Play 'People Difference': make a large set of 0–9 digit cards (one for each child); go into a large space and call out an instruction such as *Difference of 3*; the children then pair up according to the instruction.

7-UP

OBJECTIVES: To use known addition facts. To use vocabulary related to addition (such as *total, sum, equals, makes*). To choose an appropriate operation and think logically.

BEFORE: Make sure the children understand the traditional domino game, perhaps using the dominoes on page 47. Discuss how you might make a total of 7 with two dominoes.

AFTER: Replay the game with a group and ask them to explain how they decide which domino to place. Play with a different target total, such as 3.

TENS

OBJECTIVES: To know pairs of numbers with a total of 10. To use vocabulary related to addition (such as *add, total, make, equals, pair*).

BEFORE: Discuss the pairs of numbers that total 10. Use folding and unfolding fingers to show these pairs.

AFTER: Play the game in small groups and discuss the homework. Order and display the pairs of numbers

that total 10. Give each child a number from 0 to 10; ask them to make their number from interlocking cubes and then, on a signal, to find a partner to total 10. Then try allowing threesomes and foursomes.

FOURTEENS

OBJECTIVES: To add numbers to 20 by partitioning and recombining. To use known number facts.

BEFORE: Use playing cards to find pairs of numbers that make 14. Discuss the rules of the game.

AFTER: Play the game with a group and compare different strategies for adding the numbers. Ask: *What do you look for?* Sort out and order all the pairs making 14. Ask the children to describe the patterns they see. Play the game again, leaving in the second King; discuss what happens.

MULTIPLICATION & DIVISION

LETTERS IN MY NAME

OBJECTIVE: To understand that multiplication can be seen as repeated addition. To use appropriate operations to solve problems.

BEFORE: Use your own name to demonstrate the activity. Discuss the meaning of 'multiply', and make sure that the children can explain it to their helpers.

AFTER: Look at and ask the children to talk about their name-lists. Ask the children to demonstrate how they tackled the problem. Make the names into a class book. Practise the terminology: 'Four, ten times, makes forty', '4 multiplied 10 times makes 40'. Relate this to 'sets of' or 'groups of', using interlocking cubes.

TWO ROUTES

OBJECTIVES: To practise rapid recall of 2 times table facts. To see division as the inverse of multiplication.

BEFORE: Discuss the game. If necessary, show how many 2s are in a number using interlocking cubes.

AFTER: Replay the game in pairs. Which numbers are harder to cover and which easier? Why? Play 'Ten routes' with multiples of 10 and 'Five routes' with multiples of 5.

SHARE IT OUT

OBJECTIVES: To understand division as sharing. To use vocabulary associated with division (such as *share, equally, group, set, fair, left over*).

BEFORE: Start to play the game. Discuss and list the vocabulary we use when we 'share'.

AFTER: Discuss the game. Which numbers 'worked' (were divisible by three) and which did not? Play again; but this time, lay the cards face up and let the children choose which numbers to share. Mark the numbers that 'work' on a 0–100 number line or number square, and ask the children to explain what they notice. Can they predict for larger numbers?

BUTTON AND BEAD SHOP

OBJECTIVES: To understand division as repeated subtraction. To develop division strategies.
BEFORE: Model the activity by drawing items on the board and pricing them at 2p, 5p and 10p.
AFTER: Repeat the activity and discuss different strategies. Display the children's written approaches. Look at one set of items, seeing how many of these you can buy for different amounts.

DOUBLE YOUR MONEY

OBJECTIVES: To double multiples of 10. To use money to solve a number problem.
BEFORE: Discuss the meaning of 'double', and practise doubling some small numbers. Discuss strategies for larger numbers, such as splitting the number, doubling each part and recombining.
AFTER: Discuss with the children which doubles of tens numbers they know at once and which they have to work out. Display a list of the multiples of ten and their doubles. The children can play the game each day for a week, and keep a score of the doubles they know by heart.

HALVE YOUR MONEY

OBJECTIVES: To halve numbers to 10. To use money to solve a number problem.
BEFORE: Discuss the meaning of 'halve', and practise halving some small numbers. Discuss strategies for larger numbers, such as splitting the number, halving each part and recombining.
AFTER: Discuss with the children which halves they know at once and which they have to work out. Use apparatus to explore which larger numbers can be halved to leave two whole numbers.

HOW MUCH AM I WORTH?

OBJECTIVES: To see multiplication as repeated addition. To use money to solve a number problem.
BEFORE: Draw a line on the board and ask: *How much is this line worth in 1p coins?* Hold a few 1p coins along the line. Discuss the activity.
AFTER: Ask the children to talk through what they did. Discuss their findings, using terms such as: 'Eight 2s make 16.' Repeat the activity and find names that are worth the same amounts. Ask: *Can you make your name worth the same amount as your friend's?*

MULTISTEP & MIXED OPERATIONS

BY HEART

OBJECTIVES: To practise rapid recall of addition and subtraction facts. To choose an appropriate operation and think logically.

BEFORE: Use two playing cards to look at the numbers you can make by either adding or finding the difference. Start to play the game.
AFTER: Discuss the game with the children. Which numbers did they find hard to cover? Why? Ask the children to list the different ways of making each number for a class book or display. Try making 10 with three cards, using both addition and subtraction.

HIT THE TARGET

OBJECTIVE: To add and subtract several single-digit numbers to reach a target number. To understand that addition is the inverse of subtraction.
BEFORE: Write four starting numbers on the board. Ask for ways of making different numbers by adding or subtracting any of these four. Set a target number for the children to make in this way.
AFTER: Collect all the ways of making a total of 6 into a class book. Model some of the more complex ones on a number line, with addition as a move to the left and subtraction as a move to the right. Use a different set of starting numbers to make 6, or change the target number.

SHOPPING LIST

OBJECTIVES: To solve problems using money. To use £.p notation. To use the vocabulary of money (such as *change, worth, value, price, pay, cheap, expensive*).
BEFORE: Practise adding mixed amounts of coins together, and discuss what they might buy.
AFTER: Discuss the children's drawings and calculations. Groups can order the items by value. Make a 'catalogue' of items chosen; then set up a classroom 'warehouse' with 'cheque books' and forms to fill in. Set an upper spending limit.

THREE CARDS

OBJECTIVE: To use known addition and subtraction facts to solve problems.
BEFORE: Model the activity with the class.
AFTER: Repeat the activity with a group, asking them to explain how they knew the missing number. Compare different ways of working this out. Discuss the notes the children bring to school. Groups can make 'number machines' that operate on a number entered and produce an output; other children can try to guess the operation.

CREATURES AND FEET

OBJECTIVES: To use mental calculation to solve simple word problems. To use appropriate operations. To explain calculation methods orally.
BEFORE: Write a puzzle similar to the one on the sheet. Read it together; ask the children to suggest and 'prove' ways of solving it.
AFTER: Display the word puzzles the children have made up; encourage them to solve each other's puzzles. Have a 'puzzle of the day' and compare different ways of solving it.

AFTER YOU

YOU WILL NEED: A helper, two different-coloured pens and a sheet of paper.

YOU ARE GOING TO: take turns **counting** up to 100.
❏ Choose a starting number between 20 and 50, such as 32. You say '32' and point to your helper. Your helper says '33' and points back. You say '34', and so on. Carry on like this to 100.
❏ Choose another starting number and play again.
❏ Take a different-coloured pen each. Play again, but this time write down the numbers as you say them.
❏ Take your sheet of paper back to school.

BET YOU CAN'T
❏ Each say two numbers at a time – for example:
Starter, '22, 23'; Helper, '24, 25'; Starter, '26, 27'; and so on.
❏ Use numbers over 100.
❏ Find another helper and play as a threesome.

DEAR HELPER

THE POINT OF THIS ACTIVITY: is to be able to answer *Which number comes next?* questions. It is not about counting real things (as in *How many have you got?* questions). Help your child to hear the **pattern** of the counting numbers – for example: 46, 47, 48... 56, 57, 58... 66, 67, 68...

Play as many times as you both wish. This is a 'little and often' activity: the more often your child counts, the better he or she will become at it. Confidence is important: encourage your child and give him or her the chance to explain the game and choose the starting number. You can choose a harder or easier number later.

YOU MIGHT LIKE TO: play this in the car or on the bus.

IF YOU GET STUCK:
● Reinforce the 'decade' words by saying 'fifty', 'sixty' and so on with your child; then carry on counting as before.
● Try counting aloud together, stressing the 'ones' pattern: 26, 27, 28...
● Stick to the regular-sounding numbers and avoid the 'teens' numbers, which are harder.

Please sign: . . . .

MENTAL MATHS HOMEWORK

COUNTING AND ORDERING

IMPACT

BACKWARDS AFTER YOU

YOU WILL NEED: A helper, two different-coloured pens and a sheet of paper.

YOU ARE GOING TO: take turns **counting backwards**.

❑ Choose a starting number between 90 and 30, such as 67. You say '67' and point to your helper. Your helper says '66' and points back. You say '65', and so on. Carry on like this to 20.

❑ Choose another starting number and play again.

❑ Take a different-coloured pen each. Play again, but this time write down the numbers as you say them.

BET YOU CAN'T

❑ Carry on backwards until you get to zero. (The 'teen' numbers are trickier!)

DEAR HELPER

THE POINT OF THIS ACTIVITY: is to be able to answer *Which number comes before this number?* questions. It is not about counting real things (as in *How many have you got?* questions). Help your child to hear the **pattern** of the counting numbers – for example: 67, 66, 65... 57, 56, 55...

Play as many times as you both wish. This is a 'little and often' activity: the more often your child counts, the better he or she will become at it. Confidence is important: encourage your child and give him or her the chance to explain the game and choose the starting number. You can choose a harder or easier one later.

YOU MIGHT LIKE TO: Try counting backwards from numbers above 100 (such as 127) down to below 100.

IF YOU GET STUCK: Counting backwards is harder to master than counting forwards, because we do not use or practise it as often. You may be surprised how much more difficult your child finds this activity than counting forwards.

● First play the counting forwards game 'After You' (page 9).

● Try counting backwards aloud together, stressing the 'ones' pattern: 26, 25, 24...

● Stick to the regular-sounding numbers and avoid the 'teens' numbers, which are harder.

Please sign: . . . .

PILE OF 2PS

YOU WILL NEED: A dish of ten 2p coins, a sheet of paper and a pencil, a helper.

YOU ARE GOING TO: count up and back in **twos**.

❑ Take turns to pick up a 2p coin from the dish, place it in front of you and say '2'. Take a second coin, place it on top of the first and say '4'. Take a third coin, place it on the pile and say '6'... Carry on until all the coins are on the pile. If the pile falls, start again.

❑ Start with a pile of ten 2p coins, saying '20'. Lift off one 2p and put it back in the dish, then point at the pile and say '18'. Take off one more 2p, point at the pile and say '16'... Carry on until all the coins are back in the dish. If the pile falls, start again.

❑ Take a list of the numbers you have counted, in order, into school.

BET YOU CAN'T

❑ Count like this without using the 2p coins.

❑ Play this with a pile of 10p coins and count in 10s, or a pile of 5p coins and count in 5s.

DEAR HELPER

THE POINT OF THIS ACTIVITY: is to count forwards and backwards in steps of different sizes (such as twos). This is a useful mental calculation skill. You will probably find that counting backwards in twos needs more practice. The more often your child practises, the more confident and accurate he or she will become.

YOU MIGHT LIKE TO: tell your child that the numbers 2, 4, 6, 8... are known as the **even numbers**. Ask her or him to tell you some other multiples of two.

IF YOU GET STUCK:
● Try placing one 2p and saying '1p' (quietly), then '2p' (LOUDLY). Place the next coin on top, saying; '3p' (quietly), then '4p' (LOUDLY). Carry on counting in ones, but stressing the multiples of two.
● Try counting in this way using 1p coins, but piling them up two at a time. Count backwards this way too.

Please sign: . . . .

COUNTING AND ORDERING

IMPACT

COUNTING AND ORDERING

IMPACT

FILL IT WITH 1OPS

YOU WILL NEED: A helper, a few 1p coins, a lot of 10p coins, a sheet of paper, a pencil.

YOU ARE GOING TO: count in 10s from different starting numbers.
❏ Put two 1p coins inside this shape, saying '2' aloud.
❏ Now fit some 10p coins into the shape one at a time. Keep count of how much money there is inside the shape, like this: (put in two 1ps) '2', (put in 10p) '12', (put in another 10p) '22'... Carry on until the shape is filled with coins.
❏ How much money does the shape hold?

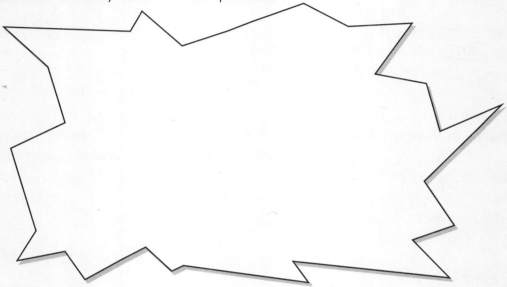

❏ On a sheet of paper, draw all the coins that fit inside the shape. Write down how much money it holds. Bring this sheet into school.

BET YOU CAN'T
❏ Start with only 1p in the shape and count in tens from that.
❏ Count the money out backwards, like this: '92, 82, 72, 62...'.

DEAR HELPER

THE POINT OF THIS ACTIVITY: is to be able to count backwards and forwards in steps of different sizes from different starting points. This is a useful mental calculation skill. The shape on this page will contain up to nine 10p coins. Encourage your child to count backwards by counting out the money from the filled shape. Counting backwards is quite difficult, but practice will help.

YOU MIGHT LIKE TO:
● Try the activity in the car or walking along the street. Say: 'I'll say a starting number and we'll count in 10s from there...'.

● Make a list of the numbers as you count (2, 12, 22...), then ask your child to identify and explain any number patterns that he or she can see.
● The numbers in the sequence 10, 20, 30, 40... are known as the **multiples of ten**. Can your child tell you some other multiples of ten?

IF YOU GET STUCK: Try starting with one 10p in the shape and counting together in **multiples of 10**; '10, 20, 30...' Then count the coins out backwards from the filled shape: '90, 80, 70...'

Please sign: . . . .

THINGS IN THE RING

YOU WILL NEED: A collection of about 30 small things (buttons, stones, small bricks or toys), a string circle large enough for all these things to fit inside, a sheet of paper and a pencil, a helper.

YOU ARE GOING TO: practise **estimating** amounts. An **estimate** is a very thoughtful 'guess'.

❑ Take a handful of the things and put them in the ring. With your helper, look at them for a few seconds. Now cover them with the sheet of paper.
❑ How many things do you think there are in the ring?
Estimate by picturing them in your head. Say something like 'About 20', 'Not quite as many as 30' or 'Just a few more than 15'. Have another quick peep if you're not sure. Then you should both write down your estimates.
❑ Now, with your helper, carefully count the things in the ring. If you want to change your estimate while you are counting, cross it out and write another one underneath. You may do this three times.
❑ Did your estimates get closer?

❑ Try again with a different handful.
❑ Take your collection of things in a bag and your written estimates into school.

BET YOU CAN'T

❑ Estimate a handful of even smaller things.
❑ Count things by grouping them in 2s or 5s (or even 10s). Does it make counting easier?

DEAR HELPER

THE POINT OF THIS ACTIVITY: is to develop your child's skill in **estimation**. Part of knowing about numbers is having a rough idea of what different amounts look like, and using that to judge approximate numbers of things without counting them. These skills develop through lots of experience of looking at amounts and being confident enough to make a **good guess**, without worrying about whether it is exactly correct. Try to use words and phrases like **estimate, roughly, fewer, too few, more, about the same as, close to** and **too many**.

YOU MIGHT LIKE TO: try using a collection of larger

objects, and one of smaller objects. Children sometimes think that if the objects are bigger, there must be more of them.

IF YOU GET STUCK:
● Count out 10 objects together with your child, then keep them nearby so that he or she can see what 10 looks like.
● If your child is still stuck, use larger objects.
● Try showing a quick glimpse of a few objects, then work up to 20.

Please sign: . . . .

COUNTING AND ORDERING

IMPACT

NAME

DATE

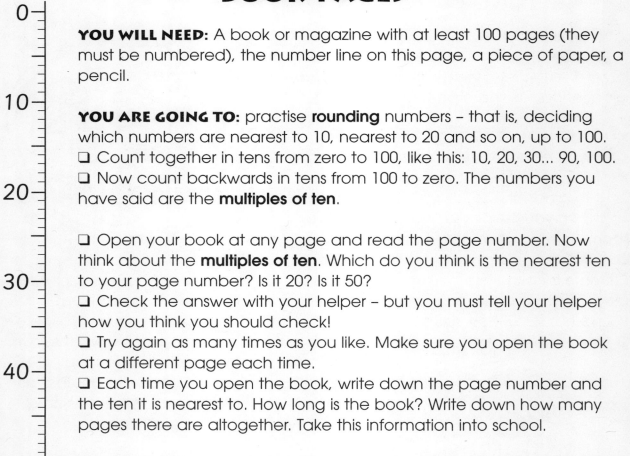

BOOK PAGES

YOU WILL NEED: A book or magazine with at least 100 pages (they must be numbered), the number line on this page, a piece of paper, a pencil.

YOU ARE GOING TO: practise **rounding** numbers – that is, deciding which numbers are nearest to 10, nearest to 20 and so on, up to 100.
❑ Count together in tens from zero to 100, like this: 10, 20, 30... 90, 100.
❑ Now count backwards in tens from 100 to zero. The numbers you have said are the **multiples of ten**.

❑ Open your book at any page and read the page number. Now think about the **multiples of ten**. Which do you think is the nearest ten to your page number? Is it 20? Is it 50?
❑ Check the answer with your helper – but you must tell your helper how you think you should check!
❑ Try again as many times as you like. Make sure you open the book at a different page each time.
❑ Each time you open the book, write down the page number and the ten it is nearest to. How long is the book? Write down how many pages there are altogether. Take this information into school.

BET YOU CAN'T
❑ Find a book or magazine with more than 100 pages.
❑ Make your own 0–100 number line and mark on it the page numbers that you have found.

HANDY HINT!
Don't forget the multiple of ten BEFORE your page number!

DEAR HELPER

THE POINT OF THIS ACTIVITY: is to develop your child's skill in **approximation**. Children need to develop a sense of which numbers are **near** other numbers in order to be able to **round** numbers to the nearest 10 (for example, *13 is nearer to 10 than 20*). To do this, they need to have a mental 'picture' of a 'line of numbers' stretching from zero (or a negative number) to 100 and beyond. Try to use words and phrases such as **nearly, close to, in the middle, exactly, roughly, round up** and **round down**.

For numbers ending in 5, it is usual to **round up** to the next ten. But it is important for your child to see that, for example, 55 is equally near to 50 and 60.

YOU MIGHT LIKE TO: have a tape measure handy to find all the **multiples of 10** from 10 to 100.

IF YOU GET STUCK:
● Children often need more help thinking backwards to the ten before. For 53, look at a tape measure: put a finger on the ten at each side, 50 and 60, and ask which looks nearer to 53. Then ask why that is.
● If your child is still stuck, try opening the book, calling out the page number and talking about which two tens it is in between. Show them on a tape measure.

Please sign: . . . .

COUNTING AND ORDERING

IMPACT

DOT-TO-DOT

YOU WILL NEED: A helper, this sheet and a pencil.

YOU ARE GOING TO: put some 2-digit numbers **in order of size**.
❏ Start by counting in ones from 50 to 100. Now count backwards in ones from 100 down to 50.
❏ Talk to your helper about dot-to-dot puzzles.
❏ This dot-to-dot puzzle is a bit unusual, as some numbers are missing.
You must still join the dots **in order of size**. The smallest number is 52. Find the dot for this number.
❏ Here are the other numbers:

85 95 71 68 54 91 63 76 58 67 79 69 80 78 59 99 64 73 97

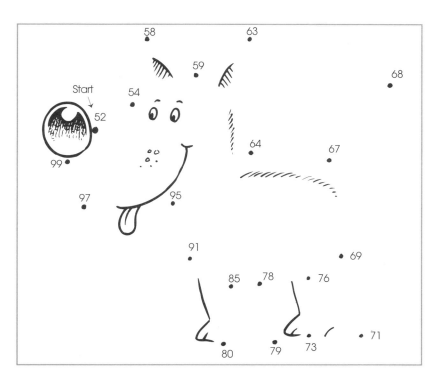

❏ With your helper, work out which numbers come next and join up the dots to find the hidden picture.
❏ Take your dot-to-dot picture back into class with you.

BET YOU CAN'T
❏ Make a list of all the numbers in this dot-to-dot puzzle and write in the numbers that are missing in between.
❏ Make your own dot-to-dot puzzle for someone else to solve.

DEAR HELPER

THE POINT OF THIS ACTIVITY: is to be able to arrange any numbers in order of size. It also checks that your child doesn't confuse numbers (for example, 68 and 86). The numbers provided are **non-consecutive**: they don't run on without a break. It is harder to order non-consecutive numbers than it is to order **consecutive** numbers such as 81, 82, 83...

YOU MIGHT LIKE TO: write out your own list of non-consecutive numbers and challenge your child to order these from the largest to the smallest.

IF YOU GET STUCK:
● Write out all the numbers in order and read them with your child. Now find them on a **number line** (a line of numbers counting up from a starting point to an end), such as a tape measure. Discuss the 'missing' numbers.
● Alternatively, write out all the numbers in the 50s, 60s, 70s, 80s and 90s in separate groups. This may help your child to order the numbers in each 'decade'.

Please sign: . . . .

MENTAL MATHS HOMEWORK

COUNTING AND ORDERING

IMPACT

IMPORTANT DATES

YOU WILL NEED: A helper, a calendar, a pencil and paper.

YOU ARE GOING TO: read some **dates** written as numbers.

❑ When is your birthday? Helen was born on 16th June 1995. This date can be written in numbers: 16.06.95.

❑ Talk to your helper about how a date can be written in numbers like that. Write your own birthday in numbers.

❑ When is your helper's birthday? Write your helper's birthday in numbers.

❑ Write today's date in numbers.

❑ Find two other important dates. Write them in words and in numbers.

❑ Now for the hard bit! **Can you put all of these dates in order, from the earliest to the latest?**

❑ Work out how many months it is between this month and your birthday month. You and your helper should do this separately, then discuss how you worked it out.

❑ Take your dates into class with you. Which parts did you find easier? Which parts were tricky?

BET YOU CAN'T

❑ Find the dates you have written in numbers on a calendar.

❑ Find out which day of the week your birthday is on this year.

Helen was
born on
16th June
1995

16 · 06 · 95

DEAR HELPER

THE POINT OF THIS ACTIVITY: is to be able to order dates written in different ways. Understanding time is difficult: there are the seasons, months and days to remember, as well as clock time in both digital (number) and analogue ('clock-face') forms. Your child also needs to learn how the different measures of time fit together: 12 months in a year, the number of days in each month, and so on. Help your child to understand by talking about events in your calendar.

YOU MIGHT LIKE TO: make up some date problems which you can solve together, such as *How old am I in months?* or *When are we halfway to Christmas?* Ask

your child to explain to you how he or she will solve each of the problems. Listen carefully to his or her explanations.

IF YOU GET STUCK:
● Try with just one month. Look together at a calendar that shows this month with all the days ordered.
● Find today on a calendar together. Look for other significant days. Write these dates as numbers for your child to read.

Please sign: . . . .

POCKET MONEY

YOU WILL NEED: A helper, plenty of coins (your helper may have enough in a pocket or purse), a pencil and paper.

YOU ARE GOING TO: count in 2s, 5s and 10s.

❏ Sort out your helper's coins (they will still belong to your helper at the end!) Do you recognize them all? Take out any 20p, 50p, £1 or £2 coins. You are not going to use these today.

❏ Count all the 1p coins.

❏ Now choose another type of coin and use them to count on from this. Count together as you drop the coins back into the purse. For example, from 5p, using the 10p coins, you might count: 5p, 15p, 25p, 35p, 45p, 55p.

❏ Now add on another group of coins, counting together. For example, using the 2p coins, you might count: 57p, 59p, 61p.

❏ Carry on counting together with all the coins, until you have worked out how much money your helper has.

❏ Now try counting the money again. This time, count all the 1p coins, then all the 2p coins and so on.

❏ Ask your helper to write down the numbers as you count. Take this list into school.

BET YOU CAN'T

❏ Work out how much your helper has in his or her pocket or purse at the start of today and then at the end of today.

❏ (This is a tricky one!) Give the coins back to your helper, **counting down** from the total amount to nothing.

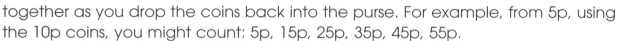

Seven 1p coins... that's 7p.

DEAR HELPER

THE POINT OF THIS ACTIVITY: is to practise **counting on** in steps of different sizes from different starting points. For example, counting in 5s from 3 gives you: 3, 8, 13, 18, 23... This activity uses coins to practise counting in steps of 2, 5 and 10. Count together to begin with. Remember that zero is the easiest starting point, and that counting forwards is easier than counting backwards.

YOU MIGHT LIKE TO:
● Discuss **how** you count on in 2s, 5s or 10s. You and your child may well find that you have different

methods of doing this. If so, that's fine.
● Discuss the pattern of the numbers: 'Four, fourteen, twenty-four, thirty-four...'

IF YOU GET STUCK:
● Start counting together from zero with the 10p coins, then the 5p, 2p and finally 1p coins.
● Alternatively, leave out the 5p coins and just concentrate on the 10p and 2p steps.

Please sign: . . . .

MENTAL MATHS HOMEWORK

IN A MINUTE

YOU WILL NEED: A helper, something to time one minute accurately (such as a cooking timer), a pencil and paper.

YOU ARE GOING TO: see how long one minute lasts.
❑ Start by watching a minute pass on your timer. Talk to your helper about what you think you could do in that much time. For example, could you write your name 10 times? Line up 15 coins? Hop 20 times on one foot?
❑ What does your helper think he or she can do in one minute?
❑ Think of a way of writing down what you can do in a minute.
❑ Try each of your activities. Write down the results.
❑ Take your results into school to compare with other people's.

BET YOU CAN'T
❑ Estimate a minute. Shut your eyes, then hold up your hand when you think a minute is up. Was your estimate too long or too short?
❑ Repeat one of your activities and see if you can do it more times in a minute.

In a minute!

DEAR HELPER

THE POINT OF THIS ACTIVITY: is to help your child start to understand and estimate the passage of time. We might say 'in a minute' all the time, but do we really mean it? Remind your child to estimate before trying the activities. By the end, your child should have a better idea of how long a minute lasts.

YOU MIGHT LIKE TO:
● Discuss how to read a cooking timer or a watch.
● Talk about how many minutes there are in one hour, and what things last for one hour.

IF YOU GET STUCK: It may be that your child is not confident about estimating. Sometimes children are worried about 'getting it wrong'. You can help by estimating yourself for the first few activities, asking your child to let you know if he or she disagrees. Make sure that you are quite a long way out when you estimate, and let your child see that it doesn't matter. You could try asking your child to write down a 'secret' estimate instead of saying it.

Please sign: . . . .

FILL THE BOX

YOU WILL NEED: A helper; three small boxes of different sizes (possibly mini-cereal boxes), or plastic containers with wide necks; a tray; some marbles, pasta shapes or other small things (all the same); a pencil and paper.

YOU ARE GOING TO: look at and compare how much these containers hold. This is called their **capacity**.

❏ Which of your three containers do you think holds most – that is, has the **largest capacity**?

❏ Discuss this with your helper to see what he or she thinks, and why.

❏ Find out how many buttons (or whatever you are using) each of the three containers will hold. First discuss how you are going to do this. You will need to put the containers on a tray so nothing gets lost!

❏ Take the empty containers and a note of what you have found out into school.

> **HANDY HINT!**
> It is easy to lose count while you are filling. Try filling the container first, then tipping the contents onto the tray and grouping them in 10s or 5s before counting them up.

YOU MIGHT LIKE TO TRY

Estimating how many marbles each container holds before you start.

DEAR HELPER

THE POINT OF THIS ACTIVITY: is to make and test estimates of **capacity**, and to use counting to solve a measuring problem. The **capacity** of a container is the measurement of how much it holds. The standard unit of measurement for capacity is the **litre** – but at this stage, children will use non-standard units of measurement such as beads and marbles. (**NB** To compare the capacity of different containers by counting objects, you need to use objects that are as similar in size as possible.)

YOU MIGHT LIKE TO:
● Discuss how accurate the comparisons are. (All measurements are inaccurate to some degree.)
● Look at some larger boxes (such as fruit juice cartons). Discuss the measurements printed on these: what do they mean?

IF YOU GET STUCK:
● It may be that your child is not confident about estimating. You can help by writing down a **first estimate**, then changing it after partially filling the container. Ask your child to let you know if he or she disagrees. Make sure that your first estimate is not too close, and let your child see that it doesn't matter. Point out that you can improve estimates as you go along. You could try asking your child to write down a 'secret' estimate instead of saying it.
● Help with counting by saying that it has to be done in an organized way. Discuss and try some different ways of doing this. Count together, rather than leaving your child to struggle.

Please sign: . . . .

ODD DOMINOES

YOU WILL NEED: A helper, a set of dotted dominoes (given on page 47), pencil and paper.

YOU ARE GOING TO: play a game of dominoes, add up numbers and look for **odd** totals.

❑ Remind yourselves how to play a game of dominoes. Each player starts with five dominoes and the rest are left in a 'pool' in the middle. Take turns to place a domino by matching the ends. When you can't lay a domino on your turn, pick up one from the pool. The first player to run out of dominoes wins.

❑ Now play 'Odd Dominoes'. Take turns to place a domino, matching the ends. Add the numbers at the ends of the domino chain together. You score 1 point when this total is an **odd number**.

❑ Keep track of your score. The first player to reach 5 points wins.

❑ Take into school a list of all the odd numbers you made.

> I have just laid 3, 3 and the domino at the other end is 1, 6. The two end numbers total 9, which is an odd number. So I score a point!

BET YOU CAN'T

❑ Play 'Odd Difference': find the **difference between** the end numbers. If the difference is odd, score 1. (For example: the difference between 3 and 6 is 3, which is an odd number, so this scores 1.)

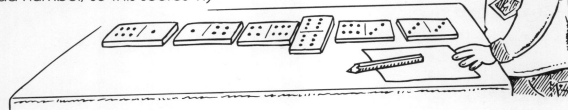

DEAR HELPER

THE POINT OF THIS ACTIVITY: is to check knowledge of odd and even numbers and to practise some addition facts that your child already knows. It also uses some number vocabulary, such as **total, add, equals, makes, odd number** and **even number**.

An **odd number** cannot be divided by 2 to make two whole numbers without having 1 left over. The odd numbers to 10 are: 1, 3, 5, 7, 9. An **even number** can be divided by 2 to make two whole numbers. The even numbers to 10 are: 2, 4, 6, 8, 10.

YOU MIGHT LIKE TO:
● Encourage your child to add up the dots instead of

counting them by saying 'Hold these in your head...' and calling out the two end numbers.
● Try turning all the dominoes face up, so that you can choose which domino to play when it is your go.

IF YOU GET STUCK:
● Try making a list of the odd numbers to 10 together, to help your child remember them. Use counters to check that a number is odd by trying to divide it in two.
● Alternatively, play the game, but add the end numbers to get the player's score.

Please sign: . . . .

EVEN DOMINOES

YOU WILL NEED: A helper, a set of dotted dominoes (given on page 47), pencil and paper.

YOU ARE GOING TO: play a game of dominoes, add up or find the difference between numbers and look for **even** numbers.

❏ Remind yourselves how to play a game of dominoes. Each player starts with five dominoes and the rest are left in a 'pool' in the middle. Take turns to place a domino by matching the ends. When you can't lay a domino on your turn, pick up one from the pool. The first player to run out of dominoes wins.

❏ Now play 'Even Dominoes'. Take turns to lay a domino, matching the ends. You can choose EITHER to add the end numbers together OR to find the difference between them. You score 1 point when you make an **even** number like this.

❏ Keep track of your score. The first player to reach 5 points wins.

❏ Be ready to talk about the game in school. Can you take in a list of all the **even numbers** to 30?

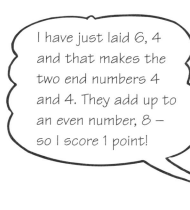

I have just laid 6, 4 and that makes the two end numbers 4 and 4. They add up to an even number, 8 – so I score 1 point!

BET YOU CAN'T

❏ Explain what you notice about adding or finding the difference between two even numbers.

DEAR HELPER

THE POINT OF THIS ACTIVITY: is to check knowledge of odd and even numbers and to practise some addition facts that your child already knows. It also uses some number vocabulary, such as **difference between**, **total**, **add**, **equals**, **makes**, **odd number** and **even number**.

An **even number** can be divided by 2 to make two whole numbers. An **odd number** cannot be divided by 2 to make two whole numbers without having 1 left over. The even numbers to 10 are: 2, 4, 6, 8, 10. The odd numbers to 10 are: 1, 3, 5, 7, 9.

The **difference between** two numbers is the amount by which one is greater or less than the other – for example, the difference between 10 and 7 is 3. Children often find the idea of **difference** between numbers harder to understand than 'taking away'.

YOU MIGHT LIKE TO:

● Discourage your child from counting the dots by saying 'Hold these in your head...' and calling out the two end numbers.

● Try turning all the dominoes face up, so that you can choose which domino to play when it is your go.

IF YOU GET STUCK:

● Make a list of the even numbers to 10 together, to help your child remember them. Use counters to check that a number is even by trying to divide it in two.

● Alternatively, play the game, but find the difference between the end numbers to get the player's score. The player with the lowest score at the end wins.

Please sign: . . . .

(grid of ten dashed boxes)

GET IN ORDER!

YOU WILL NEED: A helper, a timer, a pencil, scissors, this sheet (if you don't want to cut this sheet, you will need another piece of paper).

YOU ARE GOING TO: put some 2-digit numbers in **order** as quickly as you can.
❏ Choose a **decade** of numbers – for example, from 20 to 29 or from 70 to 79. Write your ten numbers carefully, one number in each of the boxes above.
❏ Cut out the numbers and shuffle them. Spread them out in front of you. Ask your helper to be your timekeeper.
❏ How quickly can you lay your numbers in order from the smallest to the largest? GO!
❏ Try again. Can you do it any faster?
❏ How quickly can you order the numbers backwards (from the smallest to the largest)?
❏ Take your cards and your best time into school.

YOU MIGHT LIKE TO TRY
❏ Using a different decade.
❏ Ordering the numbers from a non-tens number to another non-tens number – for example, from 27 to 37.

DEAR HELPER

THE POINT OF THIS ACTIVITY: is to be able to recognize and order numbers to 100. The numbers dealt with here are **consecutive**: they follow one another without a break (as in 81, 82, 83...). When your child has finished, read the numbers out to 'hear' any mistakes.

YOU MIGHT LIKE TO:
● Ask your child to shut his or her eyes while you read out the list, in order, with one number deliberately missed out. Can your child spot it?
● Give instructions such as *Point to the largest number* or *Point to a number in between 23 and 27.*

● Give your child some **non-consecutive** numbers (where some numbers in the series are missing) to order from largest to smallest – for example: 68, 65, 61, 58.

IF YOU GET STUCK:
● Forget the timer! Talk through the activity together, encouraging your child to look at the tens digit first and to read out each number as it is laid down.
● Count up and back together, out loud, starting and finishing in different places. Avoid the 'teens' numbers, which are the most irregular decade.

Please sign: . . . .

TARGET 50

YOU WILL NEED: A helper, a pencil and paper each, the black suits (clubs and spades) from a pack of playing cards.

YOU ARE GOING TO: make some **2-digit numbers** and compare them.

❑ Take out all the tens and picture cards (Kings, Queens and Jacks). You do not need these.

❑ Draw a line down the middle of your sheet of paper. Mark the left-hand column 'TENS' and the right-hand column 'ONES'.

❑ Shuffle the cards and put them in a pile, face down. Turn over one card from the pile. Choose here to put it: either in the TENS column or in the ONES column. Once you have picked up your second card, you cannot move your first one!

❑ Now turn over your second card and put this in the empty column. What number have you made?

❑ Now your helper plays. Whoever makes a number nearer to 50 scores 1 point. Work this out together.

❑ Play for five minutes. Who scored more points? Discuss why.

❑ Write down the numbers you make and take them into school.

YOU MIGHT LIKE TO TRY

❑ Making numbers near to a different target.

DEAR HELPER

THE POINT OF THIS ACTIVITY: is to make and compare some two-digit numbers, and to think about how near numbers are to one another. In learning about numbers, your child needs to understand the value of each digit in a two-digit or three-digit number – in other words, that the '2' in 425 stands for 20 (2 tens). This is a difficult concept: most children take most of their primary-school life to understand this for all digits in all positions (including decimals).

This is also a good activity for practising mental arithmetic – mainly adding on or subtracting 'tens' numbers. In order to work out that 35 is nearer to 50 than 66 is, your child needs to be able to add and

subtract 10 mentally to/from any two-digit number.

YOU MIGHT LIKE TO: use a tape measure as a number line to work out how far each number is from 50: count together in tens, then units, from each of the numbers to 50.

IF YOU GET STUCK: Try to make numbers less than a given target, setting a new target each time. Decide whether making a lower or higher number than the other player wins each time.

Please sign: . . . .

LOTS AND LOTS

YOU WILL NEED: A helper, some old magazines and newspapers, scissors.

YOU ARE GOING TO: look for photographs of large amounts of things.
❑ Talk about when are you likely to see pictures showing large amounts – say over 100 of something? People in crowds? Wildlife?
❑ Look through the newspapers. Cut out photographs that you think show: 10 or less of something; more than 10; and more than 50. You don't have to count them – just look and **estimate**. Sort them into three piles.
❑ You might want to spend some time over the next few days looking for photographs to add to each pile.
❑ When you have collected a few pictures of each type, discuss your photograph collection with your helper.
❑ Take your collection of photographs into school to compare with others.

BET YOU CAN'T
❑ Find a photograph showing roughly a thousand of something.
❑ Discuss possible ways of counting them (you don't actually have to count them, just discuss it!)

DEAR HELPER

THE POINT OF THIS ACTIVITY: is to give your child experience of what different amounts 'look like', and to encourage your child to be confident about making a rough estimate by sight. It also uses vocabulary related to amounts: **roughly, nearly, about the same as, too many, too few** and **estimate**.

Your child needs to have a rough idea of what different amounts look like in order to say **approximately** how many of something he or she can see – and, later, to make a sensible **estimate** of the answer when working something out. (For example: *The answer to 53 + 56 will be a bit more than 100 because 50 + 50 is 100.*) These skills develop through experience of looking at amounts and being confident enough to make a **good guess**, without worrying about being completely accurate.

YOU MIGHT LIKE TO: talk about quick ways of counting large amounts. Ask your child for ideas first. Mention that it is difficult to count the objects in a picture, because you can't move and re-group them.

IF YOU GET STUCK:
● Look at a photograph of many items and count 10 together. Look at these 10. Now use this to estimate how many there are overall.
● Still no success? Try estimating with a smaller number (up to 20 items). Allow your child to take a peep and estimate the number, then to take another peep and estimate again. Let him or her adjust the estimate while you are counting the items.

Please sign: . . . .

CLOCKS

YOU WILL NEED: A helper, pencil and paper.

YOU ARE GOING TO: discover some different ways of showing **the time**.

❏ In how many different places do you think you can find the time in your home? (Remember watches, clocks on video recorders and clocks in cars!)

❏ Find as many things that tell the time as you can. **Very carefully**, draw the time each one is showing when you see it.

❏ Which clock was showing the earliest time?

❏ Which clock was showing the latest time?

❏ Take your drawings into school. On which clocks can you read the time easily? Which clocks are harder to read?

YOU MIGHT LIKE TO TRY

❏ Discussing the picture on this sheet.

❏ Looking at a TV guide to see how it shows what times the programmes start. How long does your favourite programme last?

DEAR HELPER

THE POINT OF THIS ACTIVITY: is to practise telling the time on different sorts of clocks and clock faces. At this stage, your child may not be able to tell the time on all of the clocks in your home; but he or she will be starting to recognize hours, half-hours and quarter hours on different kinds of clock. There are two main types of clock face: **digital** (with numbers only) and the more traditional **analogue** (with hands).

YOU MIGHT LIKE TO:
● Talk about how the two types of clock measure

minutes and seconds. Watch a minute pass together.
● Talk about which TV programmes last an hour or half an hour.

IF YOU GET STUCK: The skill of telling the time needs to be talked about frequently. Take lots of opportunities when you are outdoors, or about to go out, to talk about the time and how long different activities take.

Please sign: . . . .

SUBTRACT TO WIN

YOU WILL NEED: A helper, 20 'counters' (you can use coins, spent matchsticks or buttons), a plate, a pencil and paper.

YOU ARE GOING TO: play a counting game and think **logically** about the best way to win it.

❑ Place the 20 counters on a plate.

❑ Take turns to remove (**subtract**) at least one counter, but no more than three counters, from the plate. The LOSER is the player who removes the last counter!

❑ You will need to play a few times to work out a **strategy** for winning. Discuss any strategies you find with your helper.

❑ Write down your strategy for winning on a piece of paper. Take it into school and talk about it.

YOU MIGHT LIKE TO TRY

❑ Starting with a different number of counters on the plate.

❑ Changing the number of counters you are allowed to remove from the plate when it is your turn.

DEAR HELPER

THE POINT OF THIS ACTIVITY: is to practise subtraction in a situation where your child needs to look several calculations ahead. In order to find a strategy for winning the game, your child needs to **predict** what will happen if he or she subtracts different amounts. Many children find subtraction harder to master than addition.

YOU MIGHT LIKE TO: play a version of this game without counters. Take turns to count on **consecutively** (saying the numbers in order, without missing any out) to reach the target of 21. Players are allowed to say either one or two numbers on each turn. The player who says 21 wins.

IF YOU GET STUCK: Your child may have problems with finding a stategy – he or she may just take three counters each time, or only think one move ahead. Try explaining your own turn: 'I could take one but that would leave one, two or three for you to take; so if I take three, you have to take the last one!'

Please sign: . . . .

FOLDING FINGERS

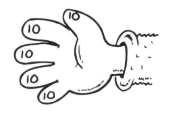

YOU WILL NEED: Your hands, your helper's hands, pencil and paper.

YOU ARE GOING TO: practise saying the pairs of numbers that make 10, and use these numbers to find pairs that make 100.

❑ Hold up both your hands. Fold down some fingers and leave the others upright. Ask your helper to tell you how many are folded and how many are up.

❑ Quickly use your hands to find **all** the pairs of numbers that make 10 like this.

❑ Now call each finger '10'. You might want to write '10' on each fingertip. What numbers can you show by holding up your fingers? Discuss how you might show 20 or 50.

❑ Now fold down some fingers. What number have you folded? And what number is still up? This pair of numbers should total 100.

I can see 3 fingers, so that's 30. So the number 70 must be folded.

❑ Take turns to hold up your hands, with some fingers up and some folded down. The partner has to say quickly what number is folded down by looking at the number that is held up.

❑ Write down the pairs of tens numbers that add up to 100 in a list, like this, and take it into class:
10, 90
50, 50...

BET YOU CAN'T

❑ Call each finger '2' and work out the numbers that add up to 20 in the same way. (This is quite tricky!)

DEAR HELPER

THE POINT OF THIS ACTIVITY: is to remind your child of the pairs of numbers which total 10. He or she then uses these numbers to find pairs of tens-numbers which total 100 – for example, 2 and 8 total 10, so 20 and 80 must total 100. At this stage, your child will be trying to learn these addition facts by heart.

YOU MIGHT LIKE TO: Write a list of all the pairs of tens numbers that total 100 in order, like this:
10, 90
20, 80
30, 70
40, 60...

Then take turns to cover one number on the list and ask the other player to say what it is.

IF YOU GET STUCK:
● Keep practising the numbers that add up to 10 until your child knows them automatically. Use 10 buttons and hide some, then ask: 'How many are showing? So how many are hidden?'
● Write down the numbers that add up to 10 as a list of pairs from **1, 9** to **9, 1**. Discuss the pattern of the numbers.

Please sign: . . . .

ADDITION AND SUBTRACTION

THREE-DICE ADDITION

YOU WILL NEED: A helper, three dice, the grid on this page, some 'counters' (such as buttons) in two different colours.

YOU ARE GOING TO: practise adding three numbers together.
❑ Start with a pile of 'counters' each. You and your helper should have different-coloured counters. The aim is to make a row of three counters in your colour.
❑ Roll all three dice and say the **total** (what all three numbers add up to). Place a counter on that total on the grid.
❑ Now your helper has a turn to roll the dice and say the total.
❑ If you make a total that is already covered by a counter, you miss that turn.
❑ Be ready to discuss what happened in school. Think about which totals seem to come up most often.

4	12	8	13
9	3	14	5
7	18	10	17
15	11	6	16

BET YOU CAN'T
Add up faster! The player who says the total first places a counter.
Play several times. The first player to place 5 counters wins.

DEAR HELPER

THE POINT OF THIS ACTIVITY: is to practise mental addition of three single-digit numbers. Your child should get quicker at saying the totals the more times you play the game.
  Take some time to compare different ways of adding three numbers mentally. For example: with 2, 6 and 3, you might say '2 and 3 make 5, 5 and 6 make 11' – **or** you might say '6 and 3 is 9 and 2 more is 11'.

YOU MIGHT LIKE TO: call out the three numbers when they are rolled. This will help your child to view them as **numbers** rather than sets of dots.

IF YOU GET STUCK:
● Play a simpler version of the game, using two dice and a grid with the numbers from 2 to 12.
● If your child is counting the dots, shake the dice in a cup, tip the dice out and allow him or her a quick peep before covering the dice with the cup. Allow a second quick peep if necessary. Encourage your child to say the two (or three) numbers out loud before saying the total.

Please sign: . . . .

DIFFERENCE DOMINOES

YOU WILL NEED: A helper, a set of dotted dominoes (given on page 47), a pencil and paper.

I have just laid 6, 3, so the two end numbers are 3 and 1. The difference between 3 and 1 is 2, so my score for this go is 2.

YOU ARE GOING TO: practise finding differences by scoring a game of dominoes.

❑ Remind yourselves how to play a game of dominoes. Each player starts with five dominoes and the rest are left in a 'pool' in the middle. Take turns to place a domino by matching the ends. When you can't lay a domino on your turn, pick up one from the pool. The first player to run out of dominoes wins.

❑ Now play 'Difference dominoes'. Take turns to lay a domino, matching the ends. Your score is the difference between the two numbers at each end of the chain. So, in the game shown above, the player scores 2.

❑ Keep track of your total score. The winner is the player with the **lowest** total score at the end of the game!

❑ Take your score sheet into school with you and be ready to talk about what happened.

The difference between 2 and 3 is that 3 is curlier.

BET YOU CAN'T

Play 'Difference 3', where the end numbers must have a difference of 3. Each time this happens, you score 1 point. The first player to score 5 wins.

DEAR HELPER

THE POINT OF THIS ACTIVITY: is to practise some subtraction facts involving numbers within 10, and to use these to solve a problem. The game concentrates on finding the **difference** between two small numbers – that is, the amount by which one is greater or less than the other. So the **difference** between 10 and 7 is 3.

YOU MIGHT LIKE TO: Try looking at two numbers and talking about the **difference** between them. For example, compare the ages of two different children.

IF YOU GET STUCK:
● Provide some 'counters'. If your child has trouble finding differences, ask him or her to make each pair of end-numbers with the 'counters' in order to see the difference between them.
● Change the game by adding the end numbers instead of 'differencing' them.

Please sign: . . . .

ADDITION AND SUBTRACTION

IMPACT

7-UP

YOU WILL NEED: A helper, a set of dotted dominoes (given on page 47), a pencil and paper.

YOU ARE GOING TO: practise making totals of 7 by playing a game of dominoes.
❑ Remind yourselves how to play a game of dominoes. Each player starts with five dominoes and the rest are left in a 'pool' in the middle. Take turns to place a domino by matching the ends. When you can't lay a domino on your turn, pick up one from the pool. The first player to run out of dominoes wins.

❑ Now play '7-up'. Take turns to lay a domino, matching the ends.
If the numbers at each end of the chain total 7, you score a point.
❑ Keep track of your total score. The first player to reach 5 points wins.
❑ Make a list of all the pairs of end numbers that total 7. Take your list into school. Be ready to talk about what happened.

BET YOU CAN'T
❑ Play '3-up', or try any other number.

If I put 6, 3 there, I score a point, because my 3 and the 4 at the other end total 7.

DEAR HELPER

THE POINT OF THIS ACTIVITY: is to practise recalling some addition facts that your child already knows. It also allows him or her to use vocabulary to do with addition: **total, sum, equals** and **makes**. Encourage your child to stop and think before taking his or her turn, and to choose appropriate numbers to reach the target. This kind of **problem-solving** is an important part of logical thinking and mathematics.

YOU MIGHT LIKE TO:
● Discourage your child from counting the dots by saying: 'Hold these numbers in your head while you look at your domino', then saying the two end numbers

like this: '**4** and something to make 7, **3** and something to make 7.'
● Try turning all the dominoes face up, so that your child can choose which dominoes to play.

IF YOU GET STUCK:
● If your child has trouble remembering the pairs of numbers that total 7, write these pairs out together before you start – or lay out 7 'counters' as a visual aid.
● Change the game by simply adding the end numbers to get each player's score for that turn.

Please sign: . . . .

TENS

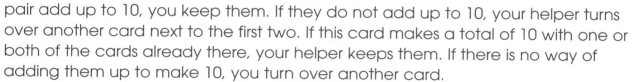

YOU WILL NEED: A helper, a pack of playing cards, a pencil and paper.

YOU ARE GOING TO: look for numbers that add together to make 10.

❑ From the pack of cards, take out all the picture cards (Kings, Queens, Jacks) and the 10s. Shuffle the cards and put them in a pile between you.

❑ Start the game by turning over two cards from the pile. If this pair add up to 10, you keep them. If they do not add up to 10, your helper turns over another card next to the first two. If this card makes a total of 10 with one or both of the cards already there, your helper keeps them. If there is no way of adding them up to make 10, you turn over another card.

❑ Both players keep going, collecting any cards that add up to 10. These may be pairs of cards, or threes, or more!

❑ When the whole pile has been turned over, look at the 10s you have both made. Write down the most interesting ways you have found of making 10 with the cards.

❑ Take your piece of paper back to school.

BET YOU CAN'T

❑ See which player can make more groups of 10 in the game.

❑ Add up the leftover cards that do not make 10 at the end of the game. Then play again. How **low** a total of leftover cards can you get?

DEAR HELPER

THE POINT OF THIS ACTIVITY: is to reinforce and speed up your child's mental arithmetic by practising recall of pairs of numbers that total 10. Being able to recognize numbers that total 10 is a very useful strategy for later calculation with larger numbers.

YOU MIGHT LIKE TO:
● Concentrate on finding the different pairs of numbers that make 10. A player scores 2 for each pair that he or she makes.

● Encourage your child to find each total by adding on from the larger number.

IF YOU GET STUCK: Try playing 'Remember the Tens'. Spread all the cards out, face down. Pick up two cards. If they total 10, keep them; if they do not, put them back in the same places. This game concentrates on recognizing the pairs of numbers that make 10.

Please sign: . . . .

ADDITION AND SUBTRACTION

FOURTEENS

YOU WILL NEED: A helper, two suits from a pack of playing cards (either all the red cards or all the black cards), a large hardback book.

YOU ARE GOING TO: practise finding pairs of numbers that total 14.

❑ Take out one of the King cards and put it aside. Before you start playing this game, read and discuss the rules.

❑ In this game the Ace is 1, the Jack is 11, the Queen is 12 and the King is 13. The aim is to use up all your cards by making pairs that total 14.

❑ Shuffle the cards and share them out between you. Stand up the book as a screen so that you and your helper cannot see each other's cards.

❑ Lay your cards out flat so that you can see them, but your helper cannot. Your helper should do the same thing.

❑ Look at your cards. Can you make any pairs totalling 14? Don't forget to use the Jack, Queen and King. Put the pairs on one side.

❑ Now ask your helper to pick one of your cards – but he or she must do this without looking! Your helper now puts this card with his or her others, and tries to make another pair that totals 14.

❑ Now you take one of your helper's cards without looking. Can you make another pair totalling 14?

❑ Carry on playing like this until one player is left with only one card.

❑ Work out why you had to remove one King, and what happens if you leave both Kings in play. Be ready to explain this in school.

YOU MIGHT LIKE TO TRY

❑ Turning all the cards face up and quickly finding all the pairs that total 14.

❑ Playing the game again, but finding pairs that make a different total.

DEAR HELPER

THE POINT OF THIS ACTIVITY: is to sharpen your child's mental arithmetic skills. The game requires him or her to practise recalling some known number facts and use these to work out some new number facts. You will need to play the game more than once before your child is able to recognize all the pairs that total 14.

In order to add together numbers that total more than 10, your child needs to be able to **partition** numbers – that is, to 'break up' a number into parts that fit easily with other numbers, making calculation easier – and then **recombine** them. For example, a quick way of adding 5 to 9 is to add 9 and 1 to make 10, then add on 4 more.

YOU MIGHT LIKE TO:
● Discuss how different pairs of numbers can be added together by **partitioning** and **recombining**.
● Ask your child to sort out all the pairs that make 14 **before** you start playing. This will show you how confident he or she is in adding numbers with a total greater than 10. Try asking questions such as: *What card do you need to go with a 9?*

IF YOU GET STUCK: Try changing the game so that your child has to make pairs that total 10.

Please sign: . . . .

LETTERS IN MY NAME

YOU WILL NEED: A helper, pencils and paper.

YOU ARE GOING TO: use your name to multiply.

❑ How many letters are there in your first name? How many letters are in your helper's first name?

❑ Both of you get ready to write your name ten times… GO!

❑ You have **multiplied** your name ten times. Now work out how many letters you have written altogether. For example, if your name is Ruth, you can find out how many letters you wrote by adding in 4s like this:

4, 8, 12, 16, 20, 24, 28, 32, 36, 40.

Four letters written ten times makes forty.

4 multiplied 10 times makes 40.

❑ Now look at your name-list. Use the example to help you work out how many letters you have written altogether.

❑ Talk to your helper about how many letters there are altogether, and how many times you wrote your name.

❑ Try again with another name.

❑ Take your name-lists into school to compare with some others.

BET YOU CAN'T

❑ Multiply your name by a different number – for example, write it 8 times. Then find out how many letters you have written.

❑ Find two names that make the same total, perhaps 30, when written a different number of times (you can make the names up if you like).

DEAR HELPER

THE POINT OF THIS ACTIVITY: is to help your child look at multiplication and understand that one method of multiplication is **repeated addition**. This is a quick way of adding the same number over and over.

Although they both give the same answer, 10 × 4 and 4 × 10 are different. Taking 4 tablets 10 times a day is different from taking 10 tablets 4 times a day! The example of Ruth's name is read as *4 times 10, 4 multiplied by 10, 4 ten times* or *10 lots of 4*. It is not *10 times 4*: that would be a ten-letter name written four times. Children may approach this activity in different ways. Be patient and allow your child to tackle it in his or her own way, even if it seems rather lengthy to you.

YOU MIGHT LIKE TO:
● Discuss how some different multiplications give the same answer.
● Discuss quick ways of counting larger numbers (in groups of five or ten).
● Work together to find out how much a pile of coins is worth by counting in groups of coin values (2, 5 or 10).

IF YOU GET STUCK: Take a handful of buttons (or similar small objects) and organize them into groups of 5 for counting, and then into groups of 2 or 10.

Please sign: . . . .

MULTIPLICATION AND DIVISION

IMPACT

TWO ROUTES

YOU WILL NEED: A helper, page 35, a coloured pencil, some 'counters' (such as coins) that fit on the grid. You and your helper need different 'counters'.

YOU ARE GOING TO: practise the 2 times table by playing a game.

❑ The aim is to be the first to make a route across the grid by covering numbers with your counters. All your counters must touch, but the route can be as twisty as you like!

❑ Take turns. To cover a number, you have to say how many 2s are in that number. So if you want to cover a 10, you must say: 'There are five 2s in 10.' If you are right, you can place one of your counters on the 10. You can start anywhere around the edge of the grid, and cover whatever numbers you like. You might even try to 'block' your helper!

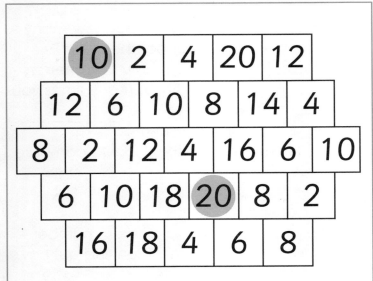

❑ To make it harder for your helper, he or she must follow a straight route and cover the next number along his or her route each time. If you block your helper's route by covering a number, he or she must start a new line.

❑ Colour in the route you have taken. Take the grid into school.

BET YOU CAN'T

Prove that there are five 2s in ten by showing the calculation on a calculator, like this: 2 × 5 = 10.

DEAR HELPER

THE POINT OF THIS ACTIVITY: is to let your child practise the multiplication facts in the 2 times table. He or she is also made to look at these facts in a new way: as the **inverse** of division facts. For example: there are 5 twos in 10, so 2 goes into 10 five times.

All the numbers on the grid are **multiples of 2** – that is, the whole numbers that result when you multiply by two. In other words, the grid contains all the **multiplication facts** for the 2 times table. At this stage, your child will be trying to memorize all the multiplication facts for the 2 and 10 times tables up to ten times, as well as beginning to know the multiplication facts for the 5 times table.

To learn number facts by heart, we need to use them again and again; playing number games like this allows us to use these facts in an enjoyable context.

IF YOU GET STUCK: Even when your child knows the 2 times table by heart, he or she may be finding it difficult to apply this knowledge to a new situation. For example, he or she may find it hard to recall any multiplication fact in isolation, being used to saying '2 × 5 =10' only after saying '1 × 5 = 5'. Seeing such a fact written the other way round (as '5 × 2 = 10') may be a new experience. To understand the 2 times table fully, children should be able to see each multiplication fact both ways round. Make a list of all **multiples of 2** and discuss how many 2s are in each of these. You could demonstrate grouping in 2s using 'counters' – for example, by splitting 10 buttons into groups of 2 and 'seeing' that there are 5 groups.

Please sign: . . . .

IMPACT

MULTIPLICATION AND DIVISION

TWO ROUTES GAMEBOARD

10

12 20 4 2 10

4 14 6 16 8 8

8 16 6 20 18 6

10 4 12 20 18 4

2 10 6 12 18 10 18

10 6 2 8 6 16

12

8

MULTIPLICATION AND DIVISION

IMPACT

MENTAL MATHS HOMEWORK

1	2	3	4	5
6	7	8	9	10
11	12	13	14	15
16	17	18	19	20

SHARE IT OUT

YOU WILL NEED: A helper, this sheet, 20 small objects (buttons, beads or little cars), the number cards from this page.

YOU ARE GOING TO: share some numbers equally between three sets.

❏ Copy the picture on the right onto a large sheet of paper.

❏ Cut out the 1–20 number cards from this page. Shuffle them and put them face down in a pile. Take turns to turn over the top card, read it and count out that number of buttons.

❏ Can you **share** this number of buttons into **three** equal sets? Try it and see. Then put the card in the right place: **YES** or **NO**. Score 1 point for a YES.

❏ Put the buttons back and let your helper have a go. Play until one of you scores 3 points.

❏ Make a list of the YES numbers and the NO numbers. Take it back to school.

BET YOU CAN'T
Predict which numbers will share into three equal sets before you try them.

DEAR HELPER

THE POINT OF THIS ACTIVITY: is to learn about 'sharing' mathematically. This is one form of **division**. The 'YES' numbers in this activity are all **multiples of 3** – that is, they are all **divisible** by 3.

Mathematical sharing activities do not happen very often outside the classroom: things in real life are more often shared into unequal parts. It is worth talking about this sort of thing with your child.

YOU MIGHT LIKE TO: Encourage your child's mental

arithmetic (when you have played for a while) by asking *How many buttons do you think there will be in each set this time?*

IF YOU GET STUCK: Use only two rings and look at the numbers that share equally into two sets (that is, are **divisible** by 2). These are **even** numbers.

Please sign: . . . .

MULTIPLICATION AND DIVISION

IMPACT

BUTTON AND BEAD SHOP

YOU WILL NEED: A helper; a pencil and paper; 3 plates; as many 2p, 5p and 10p coins as possible; at least 10 each of three types of small things (such as buttons, pencils and marbles).

YOU ARE GOING TO: see how many of something you can buy for 50p.

❑ Sort your things on to 3 plates and decide which plate might be worth 2p, 5p and 10p. Label the plates: '2p each', '5p each' and '10p each'. Make sure you have at least ten things on each plate.

❑ Look at the 10p plate. How many of these things do you think you could buy for 50p? Talk to your helper about how you could find out.

❑ Look at the 5p plate. How many of these things could you buy for 50p?

❑ Look at the 2p plate. How many of these things could you buy for 50p?

❑ Ask your helper to write down on a piece of paper how you worked out these problems. Take the paper into school for your teacher to read.

BET YOU CAN'T

❑ Invent a new price and work out how many of these things you could buy for 50p.

❑ Work out how many of each thing you could buy for 20p.

DEAR HELPER

THE POINT OF THIS ACTIVITY: is to help your child develop some methods for solving a division problem. There are several possible ways of tackling these questions: putting out 50p in coins and matching the items to the coins; guessing how many items, putting them out and counting coins to match these; working it out mentally by counting back in 2s, 5s or 10s from 50; and so on.

Never forget to give your child a proper go at solving a problem – resist the temptation to do it yourself. Give your child time to work out his or her idea, even it

seems cumbersome to you. Think how pleased he or she will be at finding the answer!

YOU MIGHT LIKE TO: Ask your child to explain his or her method, or find a different way of working it out.

IF YOU GET STUCK: Stick to 2p items; see how many of these you can buy for 10p, 20p and then 30p, working at the problem together.

Please sign: . . . .

MULTIPLICATION AND DIVISION

IMPACT

DOUBLE YOUR MONEY

YOU WILL NEED: A helper, about twenty 10p coins, a pencil and paper.

YOU ARE GOING TO: practise **doubling** some tens numbers.

❑ Put all the 10p coins together in a 'pool' between you.

❑ Take five coins and throw them all. Any which land on heads, you can keep for your score **if** you can add them up and say how much that would be **doubled**. Any coins which land on tails must go back in the 'pool'.

❑ If you get it wrong, your helper keeps the coins and you take another turn.

❑ Carry on playing. The first player to collect £1 wins.

❑ Write down which doubles you knew **at once**, and which doubles you had to think about. Take your list into school.

BET YOU CAN'T

Play with five 5p coins, add up the coins which land on heads and double this amount.

DEAR HELPER

THE POINT OF THIS ACTIVITY: is to practise doubling numbers quickly. This is a very useful skill for doing mental arithmetic. The game uses coins to practise doubling the **multiples of 10** up to 50: 10, 20, 30, 40 and 50. The corresponding doubles are: 20, 40, 60, 80 and 100.

YOU MIGHT LIKE TO:
● Help or remind your child to count in 10s.

● Observe how your child is doubling the numbers. Does he or she know the double at once or have to work it out? If your child works out the answer, how does he or she do it?

IF YOU GET STUCK: Play a similar game with 1p coins, so that your child can practise doubling numbers to 10.

Please sign: . . . .

MULTIPLICATION AND DIVISION

IMPACT

HALVE YOUR MONEY

YOU WILL NEED: A helper, about 20 2p coins, a pencil and paper.

YOU ARE GOING TO: practise **halving** some numbers.

❑ Put all the 2p coins together in a 'pool' between you.

❑ Take five coins and throw them all. Any which land on heads, you can keep for your score **if** you can add them up and say how much that would be if **halved**. Any coins which land on tails must go back in the 'pool'.

❑ If you get it wrong, your helper keeps the coins and then takes his or her own turn.

❑ The first player to collect 20p wins.

❑ Write down which halves you knew **at once**, and which halves you had to think about. Take your list into school.

BET YOU CAN'T

Play again, but **double** the amount of money in the 2p coins.

What's half of that?

DEAR HELPER

THE POINT OF THIS ACTIVITY: is to practise halving numbers quickly. This is a very useful skill for doing mental arithmetic. The game uses coins to practise halving the **multiples of 2** to 10: 2, 4, 6, 8 and 10. The corresponding halves are: 1, 2, 3, 4 and 5. When halving larger numbers, your child may use a variety of strategies. This should be encouraged.

YOU MIGHT LIKE TO:
● Help or remind your child to count in 2s.
● Observe how your child is halving the numbers. Does

he or she know the half at once or have to work it out? If your child works it out, how does he or she do it?

IF YOU GET STUCK: Your child may need more experience of halving different amounts. Try taking a handful of 1p coins and counting them together, then sharing them between you to see whether it is possible to halve the number equally. Try again with a different handful.

Please sign: . . . .

HOW MUCH AM I WORTH?

YOU WILL NEED: A helper; some 1p, 2p and 5p coins; a pencil and paper.

YOU ARE GOING TO: add lots of the same number together.
❏ Write out your full name. How much do you think it is worth in 1p coins? To find out, lay 1p coins along your name and count how many reach from the start to the end.

❏ Is your helper's name worth more or less than yours?
❏ How much do you think each name is worth in 2p coins? How about 5p coins?
❏ Draw round your coins to keep a record of how much your name is worth. Take this back to school.

BET YOU CAN'T
Find a name that is worth exactly 10p in 1p coins.

DEAR HELPER

THE POINT OF THIS ACTIVITY: is to introduce your child to the idea of **multiplication** as **repeated addition** of the same amount. It is helpful to talk through the multiplication with your child when the coins are laid out – for example, you might say: *It's worth 16p, eight 2ps make 16p.* This activity also offers practice in comparing and estimating amounts of money.

YOU MIGHT LIKE TO:
● Practise counting up to 30 and back in 2s with your

child before using the 2p coins in the activity.
● Encourage your child to estimate how much he or she thinks each name is 'worth' before finding out.

IF YOU GET STUCK: Concentrate on working with 2p coins. Tap each coin twice, saying '1, 2,' then '3, 4,' and so on as you count them up. Look at how many 2p coins make up the final amount.

Please sign: . . . .

MULTIPLICATION AND DIVISION

IMPACT

BY HEART

YOU WILL NEED: A helper, a pack of playing cards.

YOU ARE GOING TO: practise adding and subtracting within 20 – QUICKLY!

❑ Read and agree on the rules below.

❑ Sort out all the suits in the pack: hearts, diamonds, clubs and spades. The picture cards will count as: Jack is 11, Queen is 12, King is 13.

❑ Lay out the hearts in order from the Ace (1) to the King (13).

THE RULES

❑ Choose one of the black suits each (clubs or spades). Then shuffle your cards and place them as a pile, face down, in front of you.

❑ The aim is to get rid of all your cards by making pairs to cover the heart cards. Take the two top cards from your pile. You can **either** add these numbers **or** find the difference between them. Lay that pair to cover a heart card with a number that you can make. (So with a 2 and a 7, you could cover **either** the 9 **or** the 5.)

❑ You are allowed to put a pair of cards down on a heart that has already been covered. If you can't go, put the pair of cards back at the bottom of your pile and wait for your next turn.

❑ Be ready to talk about what happened in school. Think about this question: 'Were some of the heart numbers harder to cover than the others? Why do you think this was?'

BET YOU CAN'T

❑ Play with this TOUGH rule: You can only cover each heart with **one** pair of cards.

❑ Play with this FRIENDLY rule: At the end, co-operate by using both your piles together to cover as many hearts as possible.

⌐ DEAR HELPER

THE POINT OF THIS ACTIVITY: is to help your child learn basic addition and subtraction facts by using them over and over. Games are an enjoyable way to practise recall of number facts.

    Your child should be starting to add and subtract **single-digit** numbers in his or her head (mentally). See below for ways to encourage this! He or she will also be learning that there are several possible ways of reaching any total – for example, 7 is 2 + 5 or 8 – 1.

YOU MIGHT LIKE TO: Talk as the game continues about what numbers your child needs to make, and how they could be made.

IF YOU GET STUCK:

● Try using just addition, or just subtraction.

● If your child is still making a lot of mistakes, or using fingers to calculate, he or she may be under-confident and so relying on counting. Don't over-emphasize mistakes: concentrate on the correct answers, and always encourage your child to 'have a go'. Ask: *Do you know this without counting?* Try calling out the larger number, asking your child to hold it in his or her head, then **counting on** (or **back**) to get the answer. As you draw two cards, talk through what you could do.

Please sign: . . . .

MULTISTEP AND MIXED OPERATIONS

IMPACT

HIT THE TARGET

YOU WILL NEED: A helper, a pencil and paper.

YOU ARE GOING TO: try to 'hit' a target number by adding and subtracting.

❏ Your **starting numbers** are 2, 3, 4 and 5. Your **target number** is 6.

❏ You can use any of the starting numbers to hit the target number by adding and subtracting. You can **only** use the four starting numbers at most, but you can use numbers more than once. For example, you could make the target number by working out:

$$2 + 2 + 2 = \mathbf{6}$$
$$3 + 5 - 2 = \mathbf{6}$$
$$5 + 5 - 2 - 2 = \mathbf{6}\dots \text{ and so on.}$$

❏ Write down a list of all the ways you can find. Take your list into school.

BET YOU CAN'T

❏ Use the same starting numbers to hit a different target number.

❏ Only use each starting number **once** each time.

DEAR HELPER

THE POINT OF THIS ACTIVITY: is to practise adding and subtracting small numbers to reach a set total. This involves keeping a running total and adjusting it. The activity should also help your child to realize that **subtraction reverses addition**.

YOU MIGHT LIKE TO: Plot some of the moves on a **number line** (a line of numbers counting up from a starting point to an end). A tape measure works well for this purpose. You could point with your finger to show

+6 as a move six places along the line to the right, and −2 as a move two places backwards to the left.

IF YOU GET STUCK: Provide a calculator to encourage your child to try various number combinations. A calculator will give him or her the opportunity to do some 'trial and improvement' before writing anything down.

Please sign: . . . .

SHOPPING LIST

YOU WILL NEED: A helper, a selection of coins, shopping catalogues, a pencil and paper.

YOU ARE GOING TO: look at what you can buy for different amounts of money.
❑ Arrange the coins in front of you. If you could spend all this money, what might you buy? You will need to add up all the coins and discuss what they are worth with your helper.
❑ Draw a picture of what you would choose to buy. Write down beside each thing how much it would cost. You might choose to buy one more expensive thing, or two or three cheaper things. You don't have to spend all the money! Write down how much you have spent overall in £ and p.
❑ What if you could spend up to £5.00? Or up to £10.00?
❑ Look through a catalogue to see what some things cost, then choose some of the cheaper items and write down their prices.
❑ Work out how much change you would get from £10.00 if you bought one of these items.
❑ Take your drawings and calculations into school.

BET YOU CAN'T

Count up how much money there is in a money box, purse or piggy bank. How much more would you need to add to make it up to the next pound?

DEAR HELPER

THE POINT OF THIS ACTIVITY: is to look at the value of money and work out different ways of spending a fixed amount. This helps your child to apply his or her developing number knowledge to real-life situations.

YOU MIGHT LIKE TO: Discuss how amounts of money are written. For example, £3.25 means £3 and 25 pence. Help your child to write different amounts of money correctly in this way. Remember that you do

not need a 'p' at the end because you have a £ sign at the beginning!

IF YOU GET STUCK: Count the mixed coins together, talking it through. Select the higher-value coins first and add them, then write down this amount before adding up the others. Stick to finding things that cost less than this amount of money.

Please sign: . . . .

THREE CARDS

YOU WILL NEED: A helper, a pack of playing cards with the picture cards (Jacks, Queens and Kings) removed.

YOU ARE GOING TO: make up some number sentences, then work out some unknown numbers.

❏ Work with your helper to make a set of three playing cards, all the same colour. The numbers on two of the cards must add up to the number on the third card. For example:

❏ How many sets of three cards can you make like this?

❏ Now look at one of your three-card sets. Your helper will ask you to close your eyes while he or she turns over one of the cards in the set, like this:

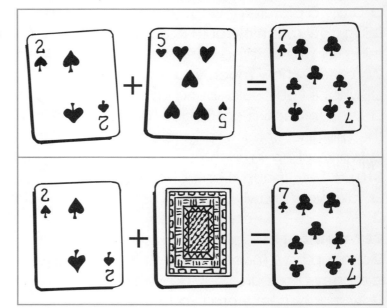

❏ Your helper will now tell you to open your eyes, and ask you which number is on the upside-down card. Turn it back to see whether you were right!

❏ Close your eyes and play again. Try it several times.

❏ Ask your helper to write down which numbers you found easier and which you found harder. Take this list into school.

BET YOU CAN'T

❏ Explain to your helper how you worked out the hidden numbers.

❏ Turn over a card, and ask your helper to work it out (you must work out the answer and keep it in your head).

DEAR HELPER

THE POINT OF THIS ACTIVITY: is to test your child's ability to use his or her knowledge of addition and subtraction facts in solving problems. An **open number sentence** such as **? + 3 = 5** can be solved using either addition or subtraction: **subtracting** 3 from 5, or **counting on** from 3 to 5.

To solve problems of this kind, your child needs to apply all of his or her knowledge about the relationships between different numbers. For example, he or she should begin to understand that if 2 + 3 = 5, it is also true that 5 – 2 = 3 and that 5 = 3 + 2. The more experience your child has of tackling this sort of open problem, the more confidence he or she will have.

YOU MIGHT LIKE TO:
● Try reading the number sentences out loud: *5 and something add up to 7.*
● Ask your child to write down some addition sums; then cover up a number in each sum for him or her to work out.

IF YOU GET STUCK: Concentrate on making pairs of cards that add up to a third card, then turning over the third card (the total) for your child to work out.

Please sign: . . . .

MENTAL MATHS HOMEWORK

CREATURES AND FEET

YOU WILL NEED: A helper, a pencil and paper.

YOU ARE GOING TO: make up some word problems using numbers.
❑ Read this together:

> **There were 2 creatures. They had 8 feet altogether.**
> **What creatures might they have been?**

❑ Can you work out a solution?

❑ Now make up another word puzzle about creatures and feet. You might want to use spiders (8 feet) or ducks (2 feet) – or even a mixture of different creatures.
❑ Which of your word puzzles have more than one solution? (Remember that 16 feet might be 8 ducks, 4 elephants or 2 spiders!)
❑ Take your best word-puzzle into class with you (make sure you know the answer).

BET YOU CAN'T
❑ Make up a secret puzzle for your helper to solve. Now ask your helper to make up a secret puzzle for you.
❑ Try making up some really hard puzzles!

DEAR HELPER

THE POINT OF THIS ACTIVITY: is to practise and apply mental calculation skills by converting a word problem into a number problem. This activity is harder than it looks! Your child will be doing addition, subtraction and even multiplication and division in his or her head. Encourage him or her to look at different solutions, perhaps involving more than one type of creature at a time.

YOU MIGHT LIKE TO: Ask your child how he or she

worked out the solution to a puzzle, and compare different ways of reaching the same answer.

IF YOU GET STUCK: Provide a pencil and paper for your child to draw the creatures and their feet. Do **not** show him or her a written 'sum' to work out the answer, as this activity is meant to develop **mental** calculation skills.

Please sign: . . . .

DOT-TO-DOT PICTURES

MENTAL MATHS HOMEWORK

DOTTY DOMINOES

MENTAL MATHS HOMEWORK

IMPACT

Dear Parent

We all know that parents are a crucial factor in their children's learning. You can make a huge difference to your child's education. We are planning to send home some activities that fit in with the maths we are doing in school. The activities are designed for your child to do with you, or another available adult. You do not need to know a lot of maths in order to help your child.

These are not traditional homework activities. It is important your child first explains the activity to you. Each activity will have been explained thoroughly in school. Then do the activity together. By sharing these activities with your child, you will be helping to develop her or his mental maths. And as a result of being given that all-important attention, your child is more likely to become confident and skilled in maths.

We hope, too, that these activities will be fun to do – it matters that children develop positive attitudes to maths. If you are particularly nervous about maths, try not to make your child nervous too! If your child is having difficulties, look at the 'If you get stuck' suggestions which are provided on each activity sheet.

After completing each activity, your child will usually have something to bring back to school. However, sometimes there may not be anything written down to bring back – your child is doing mental maths, so all the work may be in your heads!

If you have any problems with or further questions about any of the activities – or about any of the maths being covered – please do let us know at school. We do very much value your support.

Yours sincerely

MENTAL MATHS HOMEWORK